The Book of Psychotherapeutic Homework

Edited by Lawrence E. Shapiro, Ph.D.

The Center for Applied Psychology, Inc.
King of Prussia, Pennsylvania

The Book of Psychotherapeutic Homework
By Lawrence E. Shapiro, Ph.D.

Published by:
The Center for Applied Psychology, Inc.
P.O. Box 61587, King of Prussia, PA 19406 U.S.A.
Tel. 1-800-962-1141

The Center for Applied Psychology, Inc., is the publisher of Childswork/Childsplay, a catalog of products for mental health professionals, teachers, and parents who wish to help children with their social and emotional growth.

Second Printing

ISBN# 1-882732-55-3

Table of Contents

Introduction

Counselors and child therapists have found that children frequently benefit from specific exercises and activities done between therapeutic sessions— what many refer to as psychological homework.

Psychological homework can be an important part of a child's treatment plan for a variety of reasons:

1. It extends the time of treatment, much the way academic assignments extend the school day.

2. It focuses the child and his/her family on the treatment goals between sessions.

3. It involves other people in the child's treatment program. Assignments can be given in the child's system (family or community) in order to change different aspects of the child's interpersonal relationships.

4. It is consistent with psychological principles of how people learn and change, including the principles of redundancy of learning, transfer of training, and generalization.

In many ways, the use of psychological homework supports the principles of Solution-Oriented Therapy, one of the more popular forms of short-term therapy. Solution-Oriented Therapy takes a non-pathological approach to helping children, focusing on healthy aspects of the child's development, and the strengths in his support system. Psychological homework assignments can be used as a way to point to strengths and to have many of the competencies necessary to address the referring problem.

About this Book

The Book of Psychotherapeutic Homework represents a collection of the most popular workbook activities published by The Center for Applied Psychology. They are arranged in four sections, corresponding with the four basic modalities in which psychological interventions are typically constructed: Affective, Behavioral, Cognitive, and Social System. Ideally, a child's treatment program will include all four modalities—the A,B,C'S of psychotherapeutic treatment. Most of the activities in the book are appropriate for children ages 6-12, and many can be modified for children slightly younger or even slightly older. The book is spiral-bound so that the therapist or counselor can easily photocopy specific pages for his or her clients*. Activities can be done within a therapeutic session, sent home with the child to do with his parents, used as an activity for discussion in group therapy, or used as part of a classroom curriculum. There is no wrong way to use psychological homework, as long as

---

*The limited use of this copyrighted material pertains only to the original purchaser of this book and does not include permission for use of these materials in any commercial venture.

you are respectful of the child's needs, including the normal concerns about confidentiality.

Children are usually interested in doing these activities because they are fun, and are reminiscent of similar activities that they have seen in puzzle magazines or newspapers. It is important for the therapist to emphasize the "game-like" qualities of these activities, and the differences between psychological homework and academic homework. Here are some principles that you might wish to read to the child with whom you are working:

• Psychological homework helps you think about yourself and the people who are important to you.

• Psychological homework helps you learn new ways to look at your problems or concerns.

• Psychological homework is never graded. There is no wrong way to do it.

• Psychological homework is a means to an end. The "end" is helping you think and act in ways which are most beneficial to you and others. There are many other "means" to this same end. Talk to the people who care for you and are trying to help you. If you look everywhere for answers to your problems, you'll find them.

Feeling Faces

DIRECTIONS: Copy and cut out the faces on page 7 that show how you feel in each situation. Paste them in the space provided, and complete each statement.

When someone makes fun of me, I feel

_____

When someone pushes me in line, I feel

_____

If I won a million dollars, I'd feel

_____

When I forget my homework, I feel

_____

When I get dressed up for a party, I feel

_____

When I do my homework well, I feel

_____

When I see a stranger, I feel

_____

When I am lost, I feel

_____

Now paste in 10 more Feeling Faces and write in a situation or time when you feel or have felt that way.

Feelings Faces

upset	satisfied	interested	loving	affectionate
stressed	bored	pleased	thoughtful	shocked
dreamy	guilty	sick	silly	excited
embarrassed	shy	surprised	confused	smart
irritable	lonely	anxious	brave	disappointed
jealous	peaceful	tired	proud	worried
mad	happy	sad	scared	

Being Happy

Everyone wants to be happy all of the time, but that is not possible. Kids have problems, just like adults, and they have to learn to solve them and sometimes accept them.

When people are unhappy, they sometimes have to work at finding a way to be more happy. This seems like a strange idea to some people, because they think that happiness should just come naturally, like on some TV programs where everything always works out by the end of the show. But that isn't the way things work in real life.

What are some things you do to cheer yourself up when you are unhappy?

1. _____

2. _____

3. _____

What one thing would you change about your life to make yourself happier?

_____

_____

_____

Sadness

Sadness is an emotion that people try to avoid. But this isn't always possible. Humans feel many emotions, sometimes ones we don't like. That is part of our "make-up."

These are situations that make people sad:

When someone dies. When someone is sick. When you miss someone.

Can you think of a situation where you were very sad?

_____

_____

Ask three people what makes them sad. Write their responses below:

1. _____

2. _____

3. _____

Sadness is only a problem when it lasts a long time. Even if people have a reason to be sad, they must learn to accept whatever happened and go on and enjoy life.

Peter was sad because he moved to another city. He missed his friends, he missed his old room, he missed his grandma and grandpa. What would you say to him that might make him feel better about his new life?

_____

Fear

Everyone is afraid of something. Some people are afraid of a lot of things. Some people are afraid of things that they don't really need to be afraid of. Sometimes this is called "fear of the unknown."

List five things that children should be afraid of:

1. _____

2. _____

3. _____

4. _____

5. _____

These are some common things that children are sometimes afraid of, but they needn't be. What would you say to children who are afraid of these things?

The dark _____

Bugs _____

Thunder and lightning _____

_____

Getting a fatal disease _____

_____

Exploring Your Feelings

Sometimes we think that animals have feelings like we do. Grown-ups sometimes say:

You're as shy as an ostrich.

You're as quiet as a mouse.

You're as brave as a lion.

You're a fraidy cat.

You're as gentle as a lamb.

Can you draw a picture (or find one in a magazine) of the animal that you think is most like you?

Understanding Others

An important part of getting along in the world has to do with understanding how other people feel or see a situation. When you have a real understanding of how another person feels, it is called "empathy." Understanding another person's point of view is important in problem-solving and relationships.

What does this expression mean: "You have to walk a mile in another person's shoes to understand him?"

_____

_____

What have you done that made your parents really mad at you?

_____

_____

Do you think that they had a right to be mad? Why or why not?

_____

_____

Brian was ashamed a lot of the time because he stuttered. He hated to talk in public, but when he was called on in class, he had no choice.

What do you think his teacher could have done to help him feel better about himself?

_____

_____

Allan was furious at his mother. She didn't have time to help him study for his test, and he failed it. She was late picking him up for school. Now they were in the grocery store, and she was talking to a friend, while he needed to change for baseball practice. He was about to explode!

What would you do in this situation?

_____

_____

How do you control your temper when you really have to?

_____

_____

Susie was always sad because her father was very sick and was going to die. Everyone felt badly for her, but that didn't make her feel any better.

What do you think Susie could have done to help herself deal with these feelings?

_____

_____

What could other people have done to help Susie feel better?

_____

_____

What Do You Do When You Have a Really Bad Day?

Susan has had a terrible day and she is really unhappy. Circle at least five things that might have made her feel bad.

What can Susan do to cheer herself up? Write your ideas on the lines below.

Things to do today...

1. _____

2. _____

3. _____

4. _____

5. _____

Understanding the Feelings of Others

Imagine how you might feel hearing each of the comments below. Match the comment on the left to the way you think a person would feel on the right.

1. We all hate you.

2. Please join us at our table.

3. You are so skinny—don't you eat?

4. You're a loser!

5. You did great at soccer tryouts.

6. Thanks for helping me yesterday.

7. Why would anyone want to be your friend?

embarrassed

insulted

disappointed

hurt

happy

proud

angry

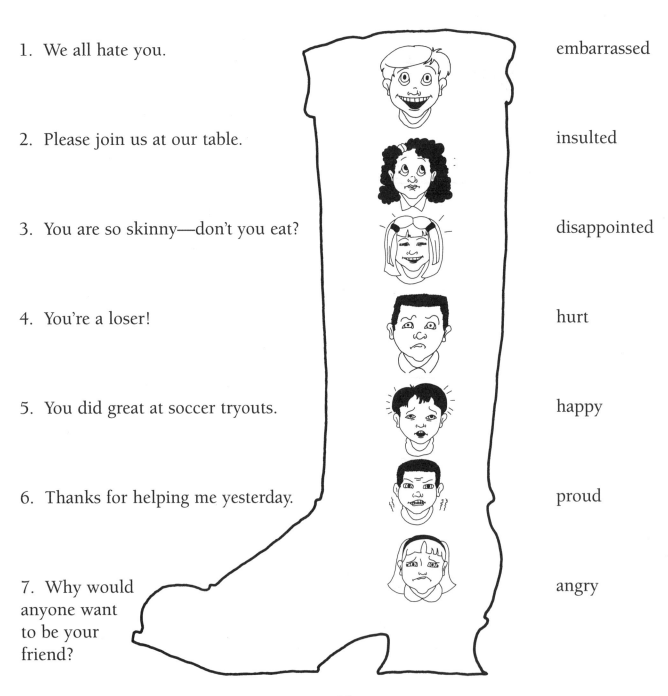

Paying Closer Attention to Facial Expressions

Match the faces that are *exactly* alike.

Now describe in words how your face changes when you are angry, surprised, confused, and happy. Use a mirror to help you if you need to.

Angry

eyes _____

nose _____

mouth _____

other _____

Surprised

eyes _____

nose _____

mouth _____

other _____

Afraid

eyes _____

nose _____

mouth _____

other _____

Happy

eyes _____

nose _____

mouth _____

other _____

The Book of Good and Bad Feelings

Get a notebook with at least 50 pages in it. You are going to make it into a "double book."

Fill in the pictures on the next page. Paste one picture on the front cover of the notebook and place the other picture upside down on the back cover. Every day, for at least two weeks, fill a page in your Good Feelings Book and then flip it over and fill a page in your Bad Feelings Book. You can write, draw, paste in pictures from magazines, or paste in photographs. That's up to you, but don't let a day go by without thinking about your feelings!

(Paste this picture on the front cover)

Things That Make Me Feel Good

(Paste this picture on the back cover, upside down,
so that you have a "double" book)

Things That Make Me Feel Bad

Growing Positive Feelings with Others

They say that good feelings make friendships grow. Think of a person you like, and then write down the things that can make you *both* feel good about your relationship.

_____

_____

_____

_____

_____

_____

_____

_____

Helping Others Feel Better

There are many ways to help others feel better about themselves. Talking things out is a good one. Write in what each family member in this picture could say to help this girl feel better.

Being Aware of How Emotions Affect Your Body

Imagine yourself as a tightly stretched rope. How do you feel as this rope?

    ____ tightly wound
    ____ ready to snap
    ____ tense
    ____ no room to give
    ____ all of the above

Now imagine your body with muscles tight, hands and feet clenched and forehead wrinkled. How do you feel?

    ____ tightly wound
    ____ ready to snap
    ____ tense
    ____ no room to give
    ____ all of the above

Draw a picture of yourself below as tense as you can get. Include whatever is making you so tense.

Learning to Relax

It is hard to feel loving, generous, polite or kind when our bodies are ready to snap. When our bodies feel this way we must say to ourselves, "I AM ANGRY" then count to ten and take gentle, deep breaths with each number you count. Relax your muscles.

How do you feel now?

Draw a picture of yourself sitting on this couch relaxing and counting to ten.

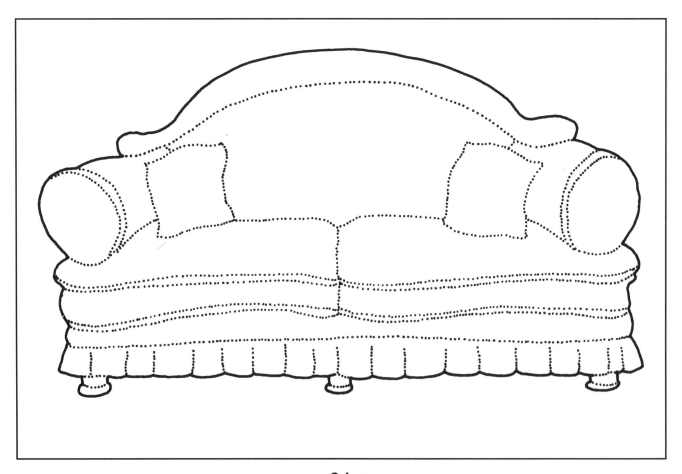

Letting Anger Go

Circle the object that rhymes with each number from 1 to 10. Try thinking of each thing as you count slowly to 10, like you are running a movie in your head!

Catching Your Anger

Angry feelings often "fly" across your mind and you are angry before you know it. Knowing what makes you angry in advance will help you "catch" your anger before it "catches" you.

Write down the five things that make you angry most often and what you can do to avoid them.

The Things That Make You Angry	How to Avoid Getting Angry
1. _____	1. _____
_____	_____
2. _____	2. _____
_____	_____
3. _____	3. _____
_____	_____
4. _____	4. _____
_____	_____
5. _____	5. _____
_____	_____

Controlling Your Anger

You may feel angry when you want something that you can't have or when someone takes something that belongs to you.

Think of the things that can make you angry. Where would you place them on your thermometer? Write down how "hot" each situation below makes you feel. What's your boiling point? Think of a way you can prevent yourself from getting boiling hot.

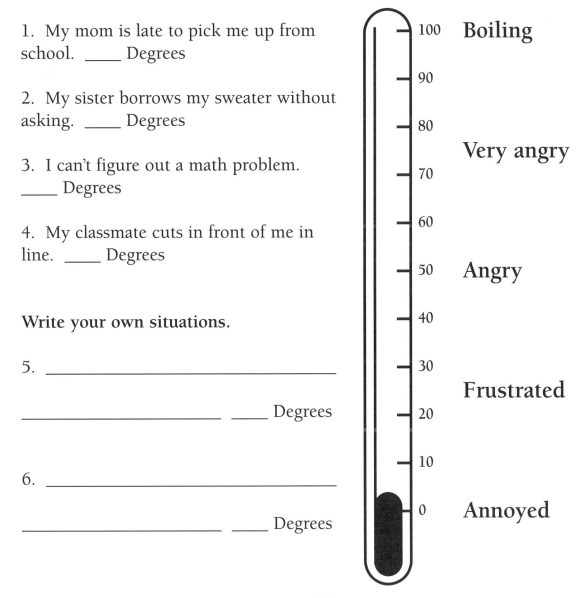

1. My mom is late to pick me up from school. ____ Degrees

2. My sister borrows my sweater without asking. ____ Degrees

3. I can't figure out a math problem. ____ Degrees

4. My classmate cuts in front of me in line. ____ Degrees

Write your own situations.

5. _____

_____ ____ Degrees

6. _____

_____ ____ Degrees

100 — **Boiling**

90

80

Very angry

70

60

50 — **Angry**

40

30

Frustrated

20

10

0 — **Annoyed**

Controlling Your Temper

Here are six steps to controlling your temper. 1.) Pay attention to your body signs that tell you that you are angry. 2.) Accept your anger. 3.) Count to ten and breathe deeply. 4.) Think of something peaceful to help calm you down. 5.) Think about how expressing your anger the wrong way will affect other people. 6.) Do something positive with your angry feelings. **Can you put them in the right order by putting the right number in each box?**

28

Understanding "Fighting Fair"

Write about a situation below where you had a hurtful fight with someone.

_____

_____

_____

_____

_____

Now list five things you could have done differently.

1. _____

2. _____

3. _____

4. _____

5. _____

Learning the Steps of Fighting Fair

Complete this maze to learn the steps to fighting fair.

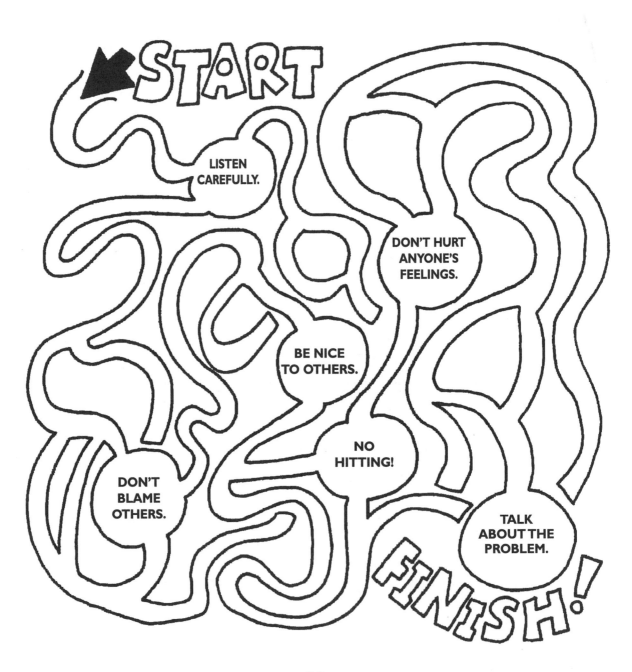

Fighting Hurts

Conflict is okay when it is handled constructively, but violence is not. Conflict is a natural part of life. Because all people are not alike, conflicts occur. It is not conflict that causes bad feelings, but the way it is handled.

In the picture below, Katie and Jeff have just had a fight. You can see what they are saying to each other. It's not very nice, and it doesn't help either one feel better. Can you write some things in the speech balloons to help them work it out fairly? Why are these better things to say?

Win/Win Situations

When people work together to figure out what the problem is, both people can often get what they want. Both people feel good, because both are winners. They have created a win/win situation in which no one loses. Look at the comic strip on the next page and answer the questions below.

What happened? _____

Is everyone happy? Why or why not? _____

_____

What are some solutions that would make everyone happy? _____

_____

Choose one solution that would make everyone happy. _____

_____

Tell what you think happened after the solution. How did each child feel?

_____

Describe a recent conflict you had where one person won and the other lost.

_____

Now write down how it could have been a win/win situation. _____

_____

Considerate Behavior

In this picture, see if you can find the things that Jane did that got her into trouble. Then, in the bottom picture, find the things she did that pleased her family.

Good Work Habits

Once Mike had a very important homework assignment. His teacher said that it had to be really neat, or he would get a bad grade. Mike really wanted a good grade, but he had a tendency to hand in work that was pretty messy. Can you help him out? List all the things on Mike's desk which shouldn't be there and what could happen.

Now draw in the things that you think Mike should have on his desk.

Avoiding Distractions

Complete this maze, avoiding things that would distract you and keep you from doing your homework.

Study Skills Checklist

Study skills are an important part of feeling in control and keeping up with assignments. Circle the study skills below which apply to you.

Classwork

1. I have my book, pencil, and paper.	Yes	No
2. I look at my teacher when she/he is talking.	Yes	No
3. I listen to directions.	Yes	No
4. I ask for help if I don't understand.	Yes	No
5. I begin my assignment on time.	Yes	No
6. I finish and turn in my assignments.	Yes	No
7. I write down my homework assignment.	Yes	No

Homework

1. I do my homework in a quiet place.	Yes	No
2. I leave my books, backpack, etc. in a special place so I don't forget them.	Yes	No
3. I turn in my homework.	Yes	No

Tests

1. I read over the material the night before the test.	Yes	No
2. I call out questions to myself or have someone call them out to me.	Yes	No
3. I go to bed on time.	Yes	No
4. I take three deep breaths before the test.	Yes	No

Circle the skills to which you answered "no." If, through practice you can change these to a "yes," notice what happens to both your feelings of success and your grades. They'll go up.

Slowing Down

Here are some words that can help you remember to take things a little slower. Can you find these words or phrases in the swamp?

SLOW   EASY DOES IT   THINK FIRST   CALM   PLAN AHEAD
TAKE YOUR TIME   RELAX

R S T I L F E A S Z O E C A
N I A O P O G C N E R T S E
G A K C A B R E L A X Q U T
I R E N A L V U T S S R Q S
Z O Y S L O W E D Y F N G M
A B O E L F X A B D G I K A
Y C U C D E Y Z C O T H E J
X E R P L A N A H E A D H I
Z T T K F Z O W K S Y I W X
P Q I L C D R O I I S T U V
O S M N B A E B P T M E Y S
M J E V R V L U B Q N P W A
E H S O L O P M L S E O I D
D F T H I N K F I R S T O R
B Q T S E I N O T A L F M M

Changing Bad Habits

Jake had a lot of bad habits he had to change. Can you look at his room and see some of the problems?

What Kind of Rules Do Kids Want?

Grown-ups make the rules. That's just the way it works. But kids often have good ideas about rules too! What are some good and fair rules that you would make if you had your own rule book? Write them in the spaces below. Do you think you should tell a grown-up about some of your rules?

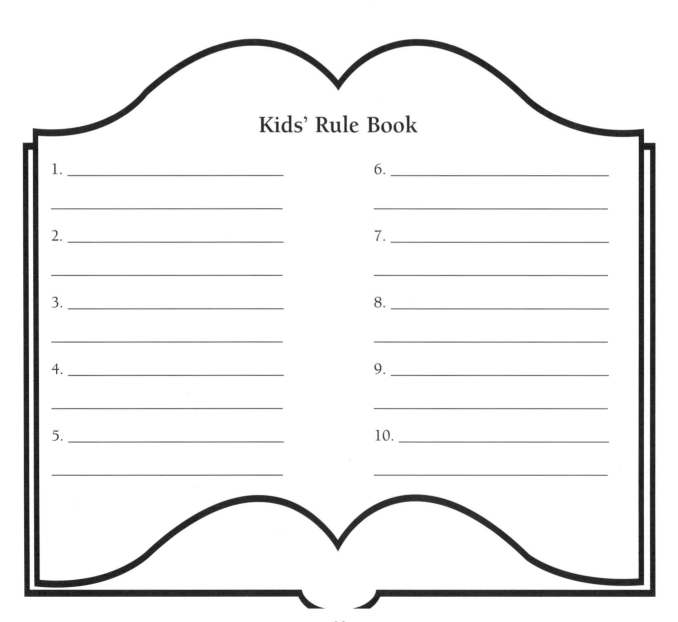

Kids' Rule Book

1. _____

2. _____

3. _____

4. _____

5. _____

6. _____

7. _____

8. _____

9. _____

10. _____

Understanding Adult Rules

Sometimes kids don't understand adult rules that keep them from having fun. Why can't Jim eat all his Halloween candy? Why can't Keisha stay in the pool a little longer if she wants to? Adults often have to put limits on children for many reasons...most of them good ones. Can you match the mixed-up scenes below? Draw a line from the boxes on the left to the correct boxes on the right to see what rules these children are breaking.

Knowing What You Are Good At

Did you know that anyone can get a perfect report card? It could happen if you got grades in what you're already good at! Fill in the report card below, choosing the things that you do really well. It could be anything, like reading or math, or playing ball or video games, or just playing! What you're good at is an important part of who you are.

REPORT CARD

Name _____

Subject	Comments	Grade
		A+
		A+
		A+
		A+
		A+
		A+

TV Watching

Most kids watch too much TV and too much violence on TV.

Do you need to go on a TV "diet?" Write the names of each show that you watch regularly below and put one "X" if it is a little violent, two "X"s if it is pretty violent, and three "X"s if it is very violent. Which ones do you need to stop watching?

MON.	TUES.	WED.	THURS.	FRI.	SAT.	SUN.

43

The Benefits of Exercise

There are many benefits to getting regular exercise. It helps you look better, feel better, and live longer. Check the activities that you do each week and put the amount of time that you do each one. Do you exercise more than you watch TV?

Activity	Time per Week
___ Speed Walking	_____
___ Riding My Bike	_____
___ Skating	_____
___ Running	_____
___ Football	_____
___ Baseball	_____
___ Dancing	_____
___ Soccer	_____
___ Gymnastics	_____
___ Cheerleading	_____
___ Jumping Rope	_____
___ Track	_____
___ Lifting Weights	_____
___ Martial Arts	_____
___ Rollerblading	_____
___ Other	_____

Whew! I feel better now!

Look into Your Future

How do you see yourself in one year from today? How are you different and how are you the same? Draw a picture of yourself emphasizing the most important differences.

Fighting Forgetfulness

Bobby was a very forgetful boy. He forgot his school lunch at least once a week. He forgot to bring his assignments home from school. He forgot to come to dinner on time. And so on, and so on.

Bobby's mother used to say, "You'd forget your head if it wasn't attached to your body," but Bobby just said, "I'll try to remember next time."

One day Bobby's dad said, "I used to be a lot like you, but now I remember everything. I never forget. I learned a lot of ways over the years to help me remember things, and now I'm going to teach them all to you." From that day on, Bobby never seemed to forget anything.

Can you find the different things in this room that helped Bobby remember? The answers are printed upside down at the bottom of this page.

Subject Organizer
"To Do Today" List
Desk Organizers ("In" "Out")

Alarm Clock
Calendar
Tape Recorder

46

Habits Learned Young
Can Last a Lifetime

Below are five children with different bad habits. They all thought that their bad habits wouldn't really affect them. . . but they were wrong.

Can you match each child with the correct picture of him/her as an adult?
(turn the page upside down to check your answers).

To Cheat or Not to Cheat

Susie had a problem. She was going to be the lead in the school play, and she had to practice every day after school. She was also the star of her softball team, and she had to play games two or three times a week. And then of course there were piano lessons, and girl scout meetings, and karate classes.

But Susie also had a book report to do and she didn't know when she was going to do it! Then one day, she was going through a box of stuff and found a report that her sister had done on one of the books on her reading list. "Maybe I could just hand in my sister's report," she thought.

Susie knew that this would be cheating, but she couldn't think of anything else to solve her problem. Can you? The answer is simple if you can figure it out.

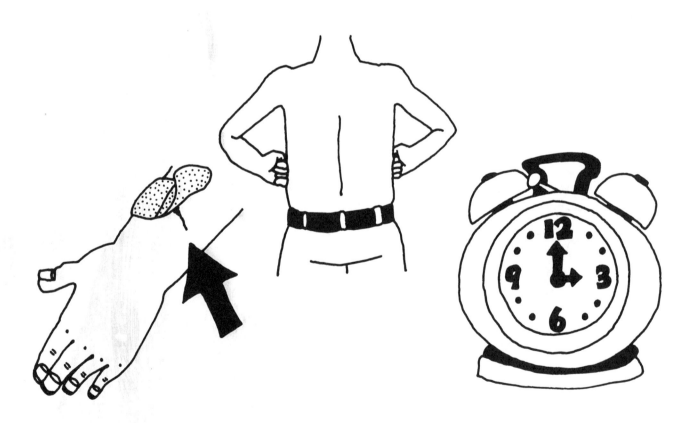

Sticking Up for Yourself

Do you know someone like Responsible Ronald? He always does his homework on time. He always keeps his room clean. He always does his chores. His parents and his teachers are very proud of Ronald. He isn't the best basketball player on his team, and he doesn't make the highest grades in his class, but he always tries the hardest. And yet some kids tease Ronald for being so responsible. They call him names, hide his books, and some kids even push him around.

What do you think Ronald would say in each of these situations? Write it in below.

Fire Awareness and Safety

There are many rules that grown-ups have that kids don't always understand. One rule that all grown-ups agree on is that children should never play with matches or fire. Fires started by children hurt thousands of people every year, and yet many children play with fire anyway!

It is much better for kids to play "fire detectives," and find things in their homes which might start fires or make them worse. **Look at the room below. Can you find nine things that could start a fire or make it spread?** (Turn the page upside down for the

Cigarette burning in ash tray.
Can of gasoline.
Jar of match books.
Smoke detector hanging open.
Overloaded socket (e.g. too many plugs).

Propane heater next to couch.
Pile of rags and newspapers.
Fire in fire place left unattended.
Iron plugged in and sitting on ironing board.
Answers:

Learning by Example

Mr. Henry is a very nice person and a very good father. He loves his children very much, and always wants the best for them. But Mr. Henry doesn't set a very good example for his children. Look at these pictures and see if you can find all the things that Mr. Henry should not be doing.

Anti-Social Behavior

Karl's family doesn't have much money so he wears his brother's hand-me-downs. The other boys in his class make fun of his old jeans and sneakers and Karl resents his parents for not making more money. One day Karl is walking around a store and decides to put a new sweatshirt on under his jacket in the dressing room. He walks out without paying for it. It was so easy, so Karl tries it a few more times. When his mom asks where he got the new clothes, he tells her a friend at school gave them to him.

What do you think will happen next?

_____

_____

_____

Have you ever stolen anything? How did it make you feel?

_____

_____

_____

Helping Behavior

Arlo's mom was sad and upset when she and Arlo's dad got divorced. Arlo began to help her do things around the house, and soon he was doing a lot of the stuff his dad used to do when he lived there. He felt good because he was helping his mother, but he was tired all the time and didn't have much chance to play with his friends or even to do his homework.

Do you think Arlo was right to "take over" for his dad?

_____

_____

Why do you think Arlo thought he should help his mom so much?

_____

_____

Was it right for his mom to expect him to do so much?

_____

_____

Was there ever a time when you did something that you thought shouldn't be your responsibility?

_____

_____

_____

Draw someone acting in a responsible manner.

Taking Responsibility for Your Behavior

Think of a problem that you had with someone else. If you don't feel ready to talk about it yet, color in the red light on this traffic light. If you think you might be ready to talk about it, color in the yellow light. If you are sure you are ready to talk about it, color in the green light. Then go talk to someone who will listen and understand.

What Happened?

What Do You Want to Happen Now?

RED

YELLOW

GREEN

Manners Matter

Jenny's mom says it's time to cut the cake, so everyone crams around the table to watch Jenny blow out her candles. Her mom takes time to ask each person what size piece he or she wants, but everyone just grabs their plate and dashes away from the table. No one even says thank you to Jenny's mom.

How do you think Jenny feels?

_____

_____

How about her mom?

_____

_____

If you were Jenny, what would you have done or said?

_____

_____

How do you rate your manners on a 1 to 10 scale, with 1 being very poor and 10 being perfect?

_____

_____

What would you do to improve your manners?

_____

_____

Do you think it is really important to have good manners? Why or why not?

_____

_____

Jim's parents are having a dinner party and have invited the next-door neighbors who are really boring. When they arrive, Jim's mom asks if he will take their coats to the bedroom. Then she wants Jim to sit down in the living room while they all talk. All Jim can think about is going to the movies with Peter later, but he tries to be polite. Jim's mom thanks him for being nice to her guests, and lets him finally go out with Peter. Have you ever been in this situation before?

_____

How do you think that Jim learned to be so patient?

_____

_____

Encouraging Yourself
with "Self-Talk"

Nobody's perfect. Sometimes you make mistakes and have setbacks.
What do you think you could say to yourself when you feel discouraged?
Write it below.

Knowing What You Value Most

If you were stranded on a deserted island but you had three things that were most important to you, what would they be? Draw them in below (or paste them from a magazine).

Using Thoughts to Control Your Feelings

Draw in a picture of a bully picking on you. Write in what the bully is saying.
Now write what you are thinking (saying to yourself) to keep yourself calm.

Bully

You

Talking Back to Anger

Some people say that when you have angry monsters in your head, making you angrier and angrier, you have to learn how to talk back to them. What would you say to each of these monsters?

Changing Negative Thoughts

Very few people want to be around you when you have a negative attitude.
Everyone likes a positive person, who talks and acts in a positive way.

Can you draw lines from the negative-thinking kid to the positive-thinking kid
in each situation?

Everyone hates me.

Sue invited me to her party, but only because she had to invite everyone in the class.

This party is fun!

I can answer this one.

Everyone thinks I'm dumb because the teacher called on me and I didn't know the answer.

I'll never be good in math.

My dad really loves me.

Wow! I got a "B!"

Dad never spends any time with me. He's so busy I won't even bother asking.

I can make friends if I try.

62

Shrinking Problems Down to a Manageable Size

1. Draw a picture of something which makes you mad, angry, or sad every time you think about it.

2. Color the picture with bright, vibrant colors.
3. If there is conversation in the picture, is it loud or soft?
4. Now shrink the problem so that it fits in the square on the next page. Does the problem seem more manageable?

Below the box, list five things you can do to "shrink" your problems.

1. _____

2. _____

3. _____

4. _____

5. _____

Visualizing Positive Images

Sometimes when things are bad, you can remember times that were really good and that can cheer you up. Whenever Charles had to go to the doctor to get a shot, he always thought about ice cream. He'd imagine that he was sitting in a huge bowl of vanilla ice cream, flowing over with sticky hot fudge. By the time he was finished taking his ice cream bath (and eating it too) the shot was all over.

What picture could you think of to cheer yourself up if something was making you unhappy? Draw it in the "thought balloon" below.

When would you use this image to help you the most?

Avoiding Problems Before They Start

Robert's grades in English have been dropping and his parents tell him that he has one month to bring them up or be punished. It's been three weeks, but he is still getting Ds on his English quizzes. There is a big test coming up on Monday, but Robert has plans to be with his friends during the weekend. He doesn't want to tell his friends about his problem, because he doesn't want them to think that he is dumb. What should he do?

_____

_____

_____

List three things he could have done to avoid this situation in the first place.

_____

_____

_____

Have you ever been in a situation like this? What was it?

_____

_____

_____

Comparing Choices

Draw a picture of something you need to make a decision about.

Now in the space below list as many solutions to the decision that you can think of. Rate them in order from 1 to 10: 1 = the decision that you think sounds best, 10 = the decision that you think sounds worst.

Rating

_____   _____

_____   _____

_____   _____

_____   _____

_____   _____

_____   _____

_____   _____

_____   _____

_____   _____

Anticipating Consequences

Do you get in trouble when you lose your temper?

___ at home?

___ at school?

Consequences are things that happen when you lose your temper. Write a story about a boy or girl who lost his or her temper below. Emphasize all the negative consequences that could happen.

_____

_____

_____

_____

_____

_____

_____

_____

_____

_____

_____

Now write a story about someone who controlled his or her feelings and thought a problem through before acting. Emphasize the positive consequences.

_____

_____

_____

_____

_____

_____

_____

_____

_____

_____

_____

_____

_____

Thinking Ahead

Owen has a habit of kicking the ball really hard during soccer games to impress his friends; so hard that he once broke a window in the church next door. The teacher yelled at him but nothing happened, and everyone thought it was pretty funny.

What do you think Owen will do next time?

_____

_____

_____

Do you think Owen's teacher should have punished him?

_____

_____

_____

Do you think it makes a difference that his friends thought it was funny when he broke the window? Why?

_____

_____

_____

Thinking Things Through

Charlie has planned an incredible ice skating party and everyone is going except your best friend, who wasn't invited. You feel badly, but you really want to go to the party. List three different things you could do to solve this problem.

1. _____

   _____

2. _____

   _____

3. _____

   _____

Think of a problem that you have right now, and try to think of three solutions.

1. _____

2. _____

3. _____

The Importance of Good Planning

Suppose you went on a picnic with your family. Use this picture to help you think about all the things that could go wrong, and then list them below. How could each problem be avoided?

Problems That Could Happen   How They Could Be Avoided

_____   _____

_____   _____

_____   _____

_____   _____

_____   _____

_____   _____

_____   _____

Planning Out Work Assignments

If you plan ahead and prepare for an assignment in steps, you are much more likely to get it done on time.

Judy knew three weeks ahead of time that her history report was due on the 20th. She didn't take the time to prepare for it, though, and when she realized that it was due the next day, she knew she was in trouble. She didn't even have the books to use for her research.

What should Judy have done?

_____

_____

_____

What are some ways to plan ahead for assignments?

1. _____

2. _____

3. _____

Think of something you have to do in the future. Now make a plan with at least five steps so that it will be done on time.

Steps   **When accomplished**

1. _____   _____

2. _____   _____

3. _____   _____

4. _____   _____

5. _____   _____

6. _____   _____

7. _____   _____

Learning Decision-Making Skills

When people need to make decisions, they usually weigh the options. They try to decide which one is the better option, even though it's not always the easiest. You can sometimes tell which is the better option by the results a decision will bring.

The kids below have some tough decisions to make. Can you help them by making a list of the consequences of each option?

A

1. "I should raise my hand and try to answer the question." 2. "I'm not sure I know the answer; I'm not going to raise my hand."

B

1. "Go to Mike's after school and play video games." 2. "Go home after school and do my English homework."

C

1. "I'll help Mom unload the groceries." 2. "I'm still watching this show; I'll help Mom later."

D

1. "I don't want to demonstrate the balance beam." 2. "I'll try the balance beam in front of the class."

A. Consequences of Option 1 _____

_____

Consequences of Option 2 _____

_____

B. Consequences of Option 1 _____

_____

Consequences of Option 2 _____

_____

C. Consequences of Option 1 _____

_____

Consequences of Option 2 _____

_____

D. Consequences of Option 1 _____

_____

Consequences of Option 2 _____

_____

Look Out for Discouraging Thoughts

Feelings and thoughts can really affect your behavior, and they can sometimes even cause it. The things people say to themselves sometimes make them act a certain way, either good or bad. The children below are all behaving uncooperatively, and you have the special power to read their minds. What might you suggest they say to themselves instead to behave more cooperatively? Write out your ideas on the next page.

Judy _____

_____

_____

_____

Mary _____

_____

_____

_____

Beau _____

_____

_____

_____

Tyrone _____

_____

_____

_____

Learning to Be Organized

Hobbies are a good way to learn organizational skills. If you were going to collect something, what would it be? In this picture, there are six common things kids collect. Can you name six more?

Friendship Awards

Each person has a special quality that makes him or her a good friend. Write the names of your friends or family under the awards that you think they best deserve. If you want, you can cut them out and give them to each winner!

P.S. A person can win more than one award.

Most Unselfish

Best Team Player

Best Sharer

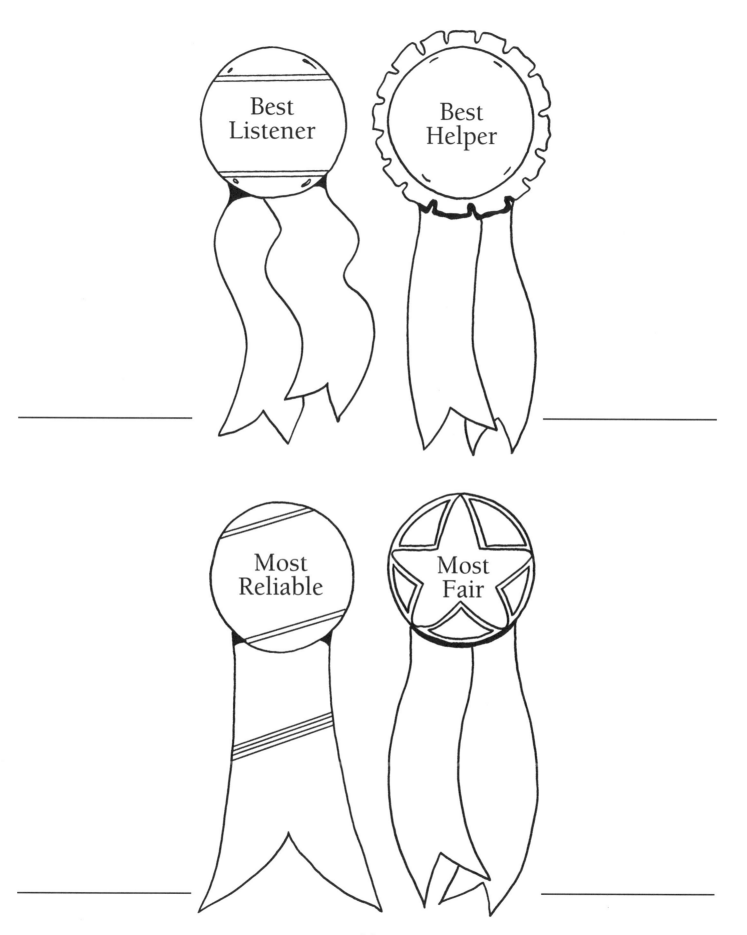

Being Responsible to Others

You probably know that you have to be responsible for yourself, like keeping your room clean, taking a bath, and going to school. But you also have a responsibility to your friends and family, and the important people in your life. When we help others, we help ourselves, too.

Below are some objects that can help you be responsible to others in your life. On the lines provided, explain how you could help cooperate using each item, and whom it would help.

The Importance of Sharing

Here's one of the best ways to be cooperative, but it's written in a secret code! Using the key at the bottom of the page, match the numbers in the top row with the letters in the bottom row to figure out this message.

$$\overline{8}\ \overline{19}\ \overline{26}\ \overline{9}\ \overline{18}\ \overline{13}\ \overline{20}\quad \overline{18}\ \overline{8}$$

$$\overline{7}\ \overline{19}\ \overline{22}\quad \overline{21}\ \overline{18}\ \overline{9}\ \overline{8}\ \overline{7}$$

$$\overline{8}\ \overline{7}\ \overline{22}\ \overline{11}\quad \overline{18}\ \overline{13}$$

$$\overline{24}\ \overline{12}\ \overline{12}\ \overline{11}\ \overline{22}\ \overline{9}\ \overline{26}\ \overline{7}\ \overline{18}\ \overline{12}\ \overline{13}.$$

26	25	24	23	22	21	20	19	18	17	16	15	14	13	12	11	10	9	8	7	6	5	4	3	2	1
A	B	C	D	E	F	G	H	I	J	K	L	M	N	O	P	Q	R	S	T	U	V	W	X	Y	Z

Getting Along in a Group

Suppose that you could start a club. What would it be called?
Who would be in it?

Club Name _____

President _____

Vice President _____

Treasurer _____

Secretary _____

Messenger _____

Other Members _____

Cooperation in the Family

Using the picture of the house below, think of some things you can do to be a more cooperative member of your household. Draw yourself doing at least four different things.

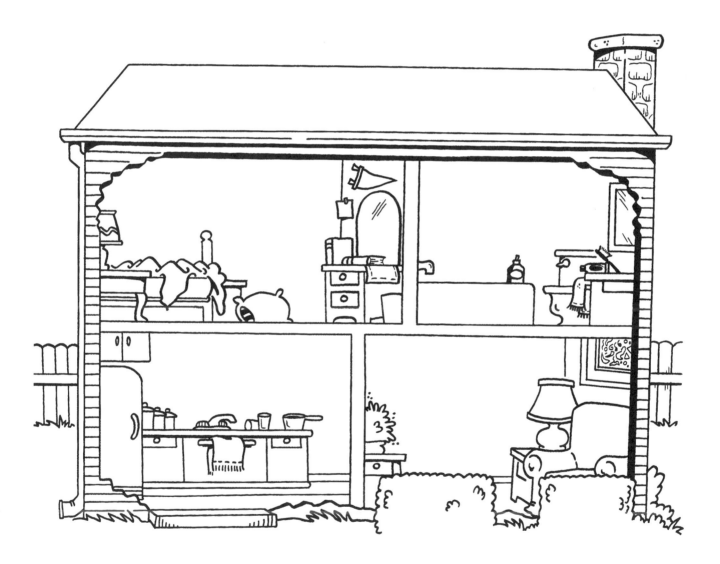

85

Friendships are Based on Things You Have in Common

What do you have in common with your friends? Cut out pictures from magazines that show activities you do with your friends. Paste the pictures in the boxes. Write a sentence about each friend and what you have in common, like the one below.

Jason and I
practice soccer.

Activities with Friends

Hidden in this jumble of letters are six words that describe some things friends do together. Circle all the words you can find. (Hint: go up, down, sideways and diagonal.)

```
W E P L A Y D E
N Z S I A X M P
L O D S H U G V
E J U T R Q G S
C A R E A M B H
E X D N F L O C
R B S A J V K I
```

Family Fighting

Bill is taking his best friend Joe for pizza with his family when his parents start fighting in the car about how fast his dad is driving. Bill's parents start swearing at each other. Bill feels like it's his fault because he picked the restaurant even though he knows his dad hates pizza. Maybe that's what has made his dad so mad. Joe's starting to look worried.

What should Bill do?

_____

_____

What do you do when you feel upset?

_____

_____

Is it a good idea to confront parents when they fight?

_____

_____

88

The Benefits of
Being Helpful

Betty is one of the happiest and best-liked kids we know. What is it about Betty that makes her so popular? Let's follow her through one day and see what she does. Below each picture, write down what Betty is doing to make other people like her.

_____

_____

_____

_____

_____

_____

_____

_____

_____

_____

_____

_____

The Importance of Family Meetings

Family meetings can be an important time to talk about problems that you are having. Most of the time other family members can help you with your problems.

Tara is having a problem learning to read. Everyone seems to be a better reader than she is. What do you think the family is saying to her? Write it in or have someone write it in for you.

Dealing With Bullies

A mean kid at school said you're stupid, and started to tease you. In the squares below, draw five ways that you could handle this situation.

Starting a Conversation

The children in these pictures have something in common. Fill in the speech balloons with some words that could draw the other person into a conversation.

When Friends Fight

Almost every friendship has some bad times. Even people who like each other very much will sometimes fight. Why do you think each of these friends had a fight? Write the reason underneath.

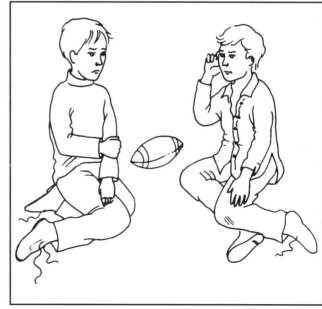

Making New Friends

All through life you will meet new people and have the chance to make new friends. But what are good ways to make new friends? Johnny just arrived from another country and started school at Maple Elementary.

These five children are each saying something that will make Johnny feel better about his first day of school. Can you think about what each one might be saying? Fill in the balloons in this picture.

Learning from Your Mistakes

Did you ever say anything you didn't mean to say? If you could talk to your friend all over again, what would you say differently? Write down what your friend said, what you said, and what you would say now.

My Friend Said:	I Said:	What I Would Say Now:
_____	_____	_____
_____	_____	_____
_____	_____	_____
_____	_____	_____
_____	_____	_____
_____	_____	_____
_____	_____	_____
_____	_____	_____
_____	_____	_____
_____	_____	_____
_____	_____	_____
_____	_____	_____
_____	_____	_____
_____	_____	_____
_____	_____	_____
_____	_____	_____

Helping and Asking for Help

It's nice to help someone learn something new, or work through a problem. You may need help sometime, too.

Name three situations when you've needed help.

_____

_____

Is it hard for you to ask for help? If so, why?

_____

_____

Albert wants to play checkers with someone. Jill sees him looking lonely, and even though she doesn't know Albert very well, she goes over to play checkers with him.

Is it ever a bad idea to help someone? When?

_____

_____

Can you remember a time when someone did an unexpected kind act for you?

_____

_____

Dealing with Peer Pressure

Margaret thinks it would be fun to try smoking one of her dad's cigarettes when he isn't home. There is a group of popular girls at school who smoke on the corner every day. She doesn't know her little sister Megan is watching. Megan always copies whatever her big sister does, and now she wants to smoke with Margaret. Megan's only six years old! Margaret feels badly about what happened. What can she do now?

_____

_____

Have you ever felt like Margaret and did something just to be "cool" or be accepted by others?

_____

_____

If you were Margaret and Megan's dad, what would you do when you found out about the smoking?

_____

_____

What's the difference between being a follower and being a leader? Can you be both?

_____

_____

Dealing with Competiveness

Mary's field hockey coach keeps yelling at her to run faster and concentrate on the ball. Mary feels like it's just a game with her friends, but it seems her coach wants everyone to compete against each other and play as hard as they can every minute. Mary doesn't want to be so competitive, so she quits the team. Her coach isn't mad, but she's disappointed when Mary doesn't learn what she was trying to teach.

What do you think the coach wanted to teach Mary?

_____

_____

Can you think of a time where you had to work extra hard at something?

_____

_____

When adults have high expectations for you, does this motivate you to try harder?

_____

_____

Understanding Friendships

Alex, Sam and Charlie are best friends and do everything together. But one day Alex gets mad at Sam and says that he doesn't want to be friends with him anymore. Sam says to Charlie, "You're my *best* friend."

What would you do if you were Charlie?

_____

_____

What would you do if you were Sam?

_____

_____

Have you ever been in a situation where you had to choose between two friends? What did you do?

_____

_____

Empathy

Jonathan always falls asleep in first period class and
looks like he hasn't brushed his hair in
days. He never knows the answer in class,
and it looks like his eye is kind of bruised.

What do you think might be wrong with him?

_____

_____

Do you think it would help to say anything to him, or should you let a teacher
take care of it?

_____

_____

List three things you might say to Jonathan to let him know he has a friend to
talk to and that you are concerned about him.

_____ _____

_____

How can you tell when someone else is having problems?

_____

_____